DREAMS

Reality

THIS JOURNAL BELONGS TO

Juliette Rose Miranda

The Awakened Seer

Introduction

Welcome to the wild, gracious and transformational realm of the dark face of the Divine Mother. Kali has been in my heart for lifetimes. In this lifetime, I remembered her at an intuitive level before I learned much about her intellectually. It is often the case with Kali that we have to feel a heart connection to her to understand her mystery.

As a goddess of fierce protection and wild grace, Kali paves the way for freedom and fearlessness. We may feel oppressed and anxious, depressed and angry, or simply intrigued when we first meet Kali. We may be attracted to her ferocious imagery because we subconsciously recognise encountering such violence in our lives and that Kali can understand us. Perhaps that violence has been experienced through abuse on a physical, emotional or psychological level. It may be a more subtle, but nonetheless devastating violence of having our humanity violated, time and time again, through labouring beneath impossible demands for perfection or an endless drive to perform or succeed no matter what the cost. There may be so much emotional backlog to be processed that we experience depression, despair, or even suicidal thoughts or self-harm, as coping mechanisms for the deep inner pain that pulls at our hearts and steals our peace of mind.

Some minds are uncertain about Kali. They may fear that she will tear them apart, causing even more violence and suffering than they are already struggling to process. Kali, with all her ferocity, tends to be the goddess on whom we project our fears of being devoured and destroyed. If fear arises in the process of working with Kali, this is okay. When we have the courage to be with all our emotional responses to her with compassion, our fears will dissolve, and we will experience greater freedom from the emotional release. Kali's most powerful blessing is freedom! She has the grace, love and power to ease the fear and pain from our souls.

It is important to remember that Kali never ever causes us harm. Her workings are on the events, circumstances and attachments in our lives. If we are fearful of Kali, it is often a sign we need to work with her so that such fearfulness within our hearts can be cleared. The question will then be one of readiness, for divine timing is very important. The right thing at the wrong time is rarely helpful. However, do remember that divine timing honours the soul. Our conscious minds may not think we are ready to deal with something when our soul and the Divine Mother knows otherwise. This is why we can trust the unfolding of events in our lives. She is fierce, yet she is pure of heart.

Kali is the mother and the saviour goddess, the protector and the healer for all suffering, spiritual darkness, confusion, devastation, disappointment and despair. She is for those suffering through violence of any kind (self-inflicted or otherwise), and those who are enduring deprivation and oppression (material, financial, emotional or physical) and need release. She is the patron guardian of those who study darkness to find wisdom and healing. That often includes therapists and people on a spiritual journey who are dealing with their woundings and taking responsibility for their 'stuff'. This work is so incredibly important for keeping the balance of light and consciousness on our planet that Kali is most generous toward people on a path of self-awareness and self-healing. She supports our progress unconditionally.

There is nothing too intense or too terrible for Kali to conquer. She is the original and, therefore, the most powerful darkness. She consumes struggle and suffering. She takes away that which inhibits our growth — and that can be painful if we are determined to hold on to it! So, she also teaches us how to let go. She teaches us to set what we think we want and need loose, and in the release, to realise that it has only been holding us back. She teaches us to let go of the things we don't want anymore and have been trying to purge from our lives, but continue to remain attached to at a deeper level, sometimes because of a wounded notion that we deserve punishment or pain.

There is no stone left unturned with Kali. We come to her when our need for healing release and freedom is so great that we are willing to do whatever it takes to overcome it. We come to her when we are ready. Even if we find it hard to let go of control, when we believe that our deepest and most profound healing and release is possible, we come to her. At a subtle soul level, she has called us. It has happened whether we consciously recognise it or not. You have this book in your hands. She has called you.

The effects of Kali's intervention in our lives is sublime. She eradicates old patterns, leaving no trace. Yet, working with her is a different experience to working with a gentler goddess (even though Kali Ma has many genuinely soft and gentle emanations, and even her fiercest emanations have pure love and the highest wisdom at their core).

It is difficult to work with Kali as her methods rarely make sense to us at the time. She tends to be swift, zoning in on whatever needs to go (typically, what we have been holding on to from a fearful place). When she enters our world, it can feel like the rug has been pulled from underneath us. However, once the spiritual storm of Kali has passed, something astonishing happens. Instead of cowering, we celebrate. We are grateful — not just that it is over, but for what has happened as a result! We realise that what she has cleared away was getting in our way. We understand that what we believed to have been a firm foundation was a false and dangerous one that couldn't have supported us. To rely upon it further would have eventually caused so much more suffering than the pain we needed to endure now to let it go.

Whatever is transformed through Kali's grace is a gift. Her transformations often appear to strike at external forms, but on moving through a Kali encounter, you will most likely find that your inner world is far more dramatically transformed than anything else. From inner changes, outer changes often flow, but the work of Kali is soul deep. She is in no way a superficial goddess, and when you open to her truly generous blessings, you can be sure you will be growing into receiving all that your heart desires. Although we are loved as her children, we are treated in such a way that we become spiritually mature and empowered beings capable of being wisdom bearers on this planet. There is no regression when working with Kali. We may go back to our childhood wounds (as mentioned, she gets to the original wounding rather than dealing with symptoms) but we will emerge as more empowered, self-possessed beings through any encounter with her.

Just like the cleansing properties of a storm, the chaos of Kali is creative and regenerative — not disruptive for the sake of it. Those who fear her tend to do so because her wildness makes her unpredictable. Those who love her do so for the same reason! Her nature is not bound by convention. Therefore, she is free to operate from a higher perspective and loving wisdom. Even though she tends not to take the softest path (unless that is going to create the best effect), she creates opportunities for the soul to take massive leaps forward that ultimately generate greater happiness, peace, freedom and joy. Kali encounters also come with the empowerment to accomplish meaningful activities that serve the spiritual benefit of all beings. She looks fierce, she is fierce (and yet so very gentle), and she always brings joy, freedom, healing and peace, in the end.

Souls who have evolved through Kali's sacred intervention—perhaps more than once—have a certain courage and the capacity to recognise the darkness in themselves and the world without being overwhelmed by it. They have a deep spiritual resting place within the soul, which can handle the truth that the path to heaven often leads straight through hell. The unexpected nature of Kali is not only her tendency for loving disruption of false order in our lives, but also the sweetness of peace, bliss and spaciousness, and the abundance and healing she brings with such gentleness in the aftermath of the upheavals we encounter. That we can discover inner light and sacred sweetness through being courageous enough to confront the darkness is an unexpected, seemingly impossible blessing. Yet, that is Kali's forte — accomplishing the impossible with her ferocious, unerring wisdom.

Kali may seem to be the one causing pain in the early stages of our encounters with her, but she does not do that, ever. She is an enlightened divine being. She has perfect divine love for us. She does not want to cause us suffering, but rather to free us from it, bringing an awareness of our pain to the surface so it can heal. If you have been trying to heal for a long time, tried many pathways and still cannot quite find the freedom you desire and deserve, here is your loving mother of last resort — although she can be your first port of call, too. Kali is so effective, so powerful, so tender and so aware of your suffering, she is absolutely trustworthy.

May every heart in need of Kali's particular grace open to her with trust and discover the joy of her blessing.

Alana Fairchild

2024 Goals

Pay off all debts

Breath

Wild

She is not quiet and subdued in the cremation grounds.
She is wild and vital. She brings energy and aliveness
to situations where there would otherwise be none.
She brings about an end to the stagnation that depletes your life force.

TAKE

Beloved Ma, Smashana Kali, Vama Kali, you raise the sword of divine truth in your right hand. My heroic heart, yearning for freedom, truth and love beyond all else, leaps with joy at the sight of you!

I offer to you all pain and fear that may arise through this process.
My heartfelt offerings are testaments to my loving trust in your wisdom.
May your power bring freedom to all beings. Jai Ma Kali!

The Divine Mother sees our capacity for breathtaking transformation and
spiritual awakening, often far more so than we recognise in ourselves.

You are encouraged to develop the confidence and commitment necessary to undertake the tasks that challenge yet also inspire you.

You will benefit from what is transpiring.

Kali Sadhana for Sacred Introversion

Sadhana is a Sanskrit word that means 'to accomplish'. It usually refers to spiritual practices that help us heal ourselves and make progress toward enlightenment. While it is absolutely possible to have limited self-healing and become enlightened, for most of us, self-healing fosters spiritual growth and makes awakening more gracious and attainable. The Kali sadhana in this journal will support you in working with the Divine Mother to make progress emotionally, spiritually, and materially, too. Kali is known to protect and bless her devotees on every level, providing for their spiritual and material needs.

These practices strengthen and empower your relationship with Kali and your higher self. They hold the promise of benefit on every level. If you need her protection, to be released, to be shown the way through confusion or to let go and clear yourself from within, then you need practices for sacred introversion.

This practice is a way to disengage from external drives and influences with the clear intention to reconnect to your inner wisdom and guiding light. Conceptualising the process as sacred demarcates it. It is an inner journeying, distinguished from experiences of daydreaming or just switching off from society (which are nonetheless helpful at times).

These processes have been created so you can have a personal and powerful method for connecting with Kali and partaking of her grace, blessings and guidance. They are an offering of the heart, made by going within to be spiritually cleansed, replenished and inspired. You can adjust them as you need, but I have taken special care, as always, with wording and ordering the processes, so each exercise is faithful to the spirit of the Kali tradition it honours. The practices are channelled from my heart connection to Kali, which led me to create many works that honour her. I hope you find the love, comfort, strength and peace that she opens up to the willing heart.

Within, you have the power of the Divine Mother's wisdom and blessing.
Do not underestimate her. Do not underestimate yourself.

She is Kripadhara, the vessel of compassion. We can go to her and receive as much love, support, kindness, compassion, protection and anything else we need.

Even more than I, you know my capacity and how to evoke my potential into expression. With perfect trust in your wisdom, I shall not turn away from what is before me. I shall successfully navigate and triumph over all soul challenges, through your grace, for the spiritual benefit of all beings.

Do not be afraid of uncertainty. If you feel you are without resources,
take comfort now. Where there is lack, she restores abundance.

Cast off your fears. Hers is the power of the Universe,
combined with the generosity of grace.

Her love will always find a way. If the way does not yet exist, it shall be created.

When you cannot see or feel how to move from where you are now to where you want to be, Kali's wisdom and grace will manifest at the perfect time to provide what you need.

Why do we need spiritual protection?

Kali is the supreme spiritual protection. Sometimes aspirants wonder:
If everything is divine, and divine love is at the fundamental essence of all
of creation, then why do we need spiritual protection at all?

*There is a story in the Hindu tradition about a man receiving teachings
from a great sage. The sage taught him that the Divine is in all things. The
group was pondering this when suddenly, a loud voice called out, warning
them to get out of the way because a wild elephant was stampeding through
the jungle. As they ran to hide, one student remembered the teachings he
had just received and instead of hiding, bowed down before the elephant,
honouring his divine nature. He was trampled on and severely injured as
the elephant rampaged forward.*

*We cannot always know why the Divine would manifest as a stampeding
elephant, but we can recognise that there is some purpose to it and respond
with awe and a swift-footed relocation to safer ground. As the Kali-adoring
mystic, Sri Ramakrishna, taught: "You can know that the wild tiger is a
divine being, but it isn't wise to attempt to hug it on that account!"*

*So, we call on Kali to help us have the compassionate insight to recognise
divinity in all beings, while also having the wisdom to know how to respond
appropriately in the circumstances.*

When nothing appears to be happening in your outer world,
there can be much of value taking place at an inner level.

She reminds us that nothing is ever hopeless, no matter how much the mind may believe it to be. Through trust in her, we become an active expression of the solution to any difficulty in our world.

We can trust in her timing and our process.
Stay true to your inner work and know
that your efforts shall bear fruit.

Through her carefully chosen life lessons, the heart becomes spiritually prepared to dispense with mainstream consciousness. The inner spiritual eye flutters open and new realities become available.

She will not allow you to be misled. If you have wandered from your path,
she will re-establish you in your authentic and joyful way to freedom.

When your plans suddenly seem thwarted, ask whether it would take more courage and growth to rise above the obstacles and continue on your current path or to step away from your initial goals and be open to a different direction.

We can discern authentic spiritual guidance from its effect.
It brings a sense of relief, even if the path ahead seems challenging.

It is not necessary to seek the hardest path, assuming it will always yield the greatest growth. Kali demands that we find our courage, but being brave may mean letting go of harshness and allowing for softness.

Honouring Kali Nitya

Kali Nitya is the cycle of the waning moon, from the moment after fullness into decline. This is the natural magic inherent in letting go and allowing energies to run their course and die away. This phase can signify the embrace of qualities of decrease for a period to bring a cycle of experience to completion and generate what is necessary for the next cycle to be more abundant and nourishing. Given our societal preoccupation with constant activity and outwardly driven connection, honouring Nitya Kali requires the use of our will to honour our soul rhythms above peer pressure.

The fifteen nityas of Kali are the divine feminine beings represented by, and honoured upon, each of the fifteen nights of the waning and dark moon. You can say the honouring statements for each of the Nitya Devi of Kali that follow. You can do this in one ritual at any time of your choosing, or you may wish to consult an ephemeris and begin on the evening following the next full moon. Harmonising your practice to start the day after the full moon is a powerful alignment between inner intention and outer circumstances which can enhance your experience. However, the intention and devotion provide the power of a practice, more so than the timing. This is not to discount the importance of divine timing and even of planetary movements and the effect such things have in human lives. It is more an honouring testament to the power of Kali's grace. She is the devourer of time. She will not let something mundane—such as it not being the right time of the month—prevent a powerful connection between your heart and hers!

You can say the prayer for each goddess before you sleep on fifteen consecutive nights or in one in-depth practice. This process will create a sacred container and enhance the release of what has been to clear the way. It will powerfully regenerate you to open up to increased receptivity, abundance and divine delight in the cycle that follows from new moon to full moon (whether that new cycle is literal or spiritual).

Sacred Practice with Kali Nitya

Place your hands in prayer before your heart. Take a moment to connect within. Imagine, sense, feel or intend that you are dropping peacefully and deeply into a vast inner spaciousness. As you go within, following the inhalation and dropping deeper on the exhalation, feel yourself effortlessly letting go of the external world and your day-to-day concerns. You are crossing the inner threshold into sacred introversion and healing presence.

Begin with hands in prayer as you connect to your inner being. Intend to open up, let go and experience healing and growth. Say the following prayer aloud:

> *In these sacred depths, your wisdom effortlessly touches my soul. I do not need to think or control. I choose to simply be here with you now and receive your subtle inner infusions of grace, wisdom and cosmic realignment. For the spiritual benefit of all beings, Jai Ma Kali!*

Proceed to honour one or more goddesses. Repeat the opening portion of this practice each night if you are honouring one goddess per evening, or just once if you are honouring all goddesses in a single sitting.

Place your hands in prayer at your heart as a sign of respect, and express your chosen invocation(s) from the practices below.

When you have said your selected invocation(s), exhale fully. Hold the intention to let go in body, mind and soul. With your hands in prayer at your heart, bow your head, surrender and submit to the loving wild wisdom of the Divine Feminine in this form. Let your hands hang loosely at your sides as a symbol of letting go and releasing.

You have completed your sacred ritual of invocation. Sense the fulfilment of the practice wrapping around you in a blessing of grace. This grace benefits all beings.

Kali Nitya Invocations

Night One:

Jai Ma Kali. Please bless me with your sacred holding and protection so that I may willingly enter the depths of my true nature, to be undone and reborn, for the spiritual benefit of all beings. Jai Ma Kali!

Night Two:

Jai Ma Kapalini, bearer of skulls. I honour that which has run its course and with courage, reconnect with the parts of me buried under distraction and denial, for the spiritual benefit of all beings. Jai Ma Kali!

Night Three:

Jai Ma Kulla, priestess of reflection, may the black mirror of lunar wisdom that reveals deeper truths show me what I need to see and acknowledge now, for the spiritual benefit of all beings. Jai Ma Kali!

Night Four:

Jai Ma Kurukulla, dakini of magnetism and sorceress of divine enchantment, as I dispense with conditioning and drop into the depths of my authentic heart presence, I attract that which brings my sacred yearnings to fruition, for the spiritual benefit of all beings. Jai Ma Kali!

Night Five:

Jai Ma Virodhini, nitya of acceptance, I embrace your gift and accept myself fully, which allows me to connect with and express my truest desires and most heartfelt prayers. I do so now with trust, for the spiritual benefit of all beings. Jai Ma Kali!

Night Six::

Jai Ma Vipracitta, goddess of the deeper subconscious and creative mind, I surrender logic and attachment to previous plans, allowing for new ideas and sacred inspirations to guide me along improved pathways, for the spiritual benefit of all beings. Jai Ma Kali!

Night Seven:

Jai Ma Ugra Mata, I call upon your fierceness and refusal to be oppressed, so that I may stand up to resistance, inner and outer, and to protect the new wisdoms awakening within. For the spiritual benefit of all beings, Jai Ma Kali!

Night Eight:

Jai Ma Ugraprabha, she who creates capacity and space for sacred introversion. I journey inward, seeking the truth within my being, open to whatever I shall discover with complete trust. This brings spiritual benefit to all beings. Jai Ma Kali!

Night Nine:

Jai Ma Dipa, she who illuminates. In my compassionate openness, having dispensed with preconceived ideas, I am ready to witness, to see and to know that which places me firmly on the path of truth. For the spiritual benefit of all beings, Jai Ma Kali!

Night Ten:

Jai Ma Nila, I embrace your power of contemplation, allowing that which has been stirring to be fully revealed and understood under your gentle, steady, inner contemplative gaze. I do not need to rush or force anything; but rather, allow the wisdom to become known. For the spiritual benefit of all beings, Jai Ma Kali!

Night Eleven:

Jai Ma Ghana, your power of divine destruction infuses me with will and clarity to terminate that which must no longer be in my life. I release, and with gentleness and firmness of spirit, I purge, for the spiritual benefit of all beings. Jai Ma Kali!

Night Twelve:

Jai Ma Balaka, mother of indulgence, she who reminds me to let others be as I tend to my own inner nature as though she were a queen worthy of greatest tenderness, devotion and attention. I give to myself freely, absolutely and completely, for the spiritual benefit of all beings. Jai Ma Kali!

Night Thirteen:

Jai Ma Matra, I am awakened to your gift of self-knowledge as I recognise my true needs and value, my purpose and my path. I am self-aware for the spiritual benefit of all beings. Jai Ma Kali!

Night Fourteen:

Jai Ma Mudra, goddess of expression, I welcome your powerful protection of body, mind and soul by assuming inner and outer postures that cultivate positive energy. With a joyful heart and peaceful mind, I am protected from unfavourable energies, for the spiritual benefit of all beings. Jai Ma Kali!

Night Fifteen:

Jai Ma Mita, you are fearless and free, and I play with your presence in my wild soul. I am emptied completely and aligned with divine grace, protected in spaciousness and grounded in readiness and presence for what shall unfold. For the spiritual benefit of all beings, Jai Ma Kali!

*She is the inoculating tonic of authenticity. Authenticity keeps us
dialled into our true purpose and passion. She protects the soul from
the castrating conventionality that steals away our creative fire.*

She is the divine disruption that provides needed, yet often unanticipated,
spiritual recalibration.

*When we stray from our authentic nature, she brings us back to the spiritual home
of the heart. She reminds us that we are most powerful and most protected when
we seek the truth of the heart — because that is when we are closest to her.*

Dispense with the need to placate others or control situations.
She has arisen and can be trusted unconditionally.

Take refuge in her and allow the circumstances of your life to unfold as they will, acting when you feel guided to do so, having patience in the unfolding events and trusting that her grace is unlimited.

She is watching over profound healing, taking place within your soul.

The spiritual cleansing and protection needed to overcome obstacles
shall be granted to you.

*You may not understand her wisdom nor her method, but you can trust in what is
happening in your life, especially the things breaking apart or arising anew.*

Any pain you may be experiencing now
is far less than the pain that would have taken root
if certain circumstances were allowed to continue.

When you feel as though the way forward is blocked, her presence indicates that spiritual intervention is imminent. No obstacle can withstand her will.

Do not avoid setting boundaries. Nor is it wise to pander to those attempting to exploit your good nature. Trying to cultivate behaviours that are not self-honouring to keep the peace in some way, will backfire. Honour yourself as her spiritual child, worthy of respect.

Trust in her more than you trust in your doubts or fears.
She has the power to bring about what needs to occur.

She appears fierce, and yet she is benign. Her oracle brings the message that a situation that may frighten or intimidate you is well within your capacity to handle.

No matter how dramatic or intense the situation may appear,
it shall eventually be little more than a passing memory
and shall have no negative bearing upon your future.

Kali Yantra and Mudra Practice to Banish Negative Interference

The body and mind can be living cauldrons through which Kali's divine magic manifests in our lives and our world. As we learn to drop our limited viewpoints, opening our hearts to merge spiritually with Kali, we can become the vessels that receive and channel her *shakti*, or 'enlightened activity', in the world for the greater good. The divine being of Kali is not simply an idea or metaphor. Her presence is a real, living power. We can awaken to living within the temple of her being, even as we go about our daily lives. We can experience her as always being with us.

When we approach the sacred geometric symbol known as a yantra, we are approaching a powerful, symbolic and actual portal into the Universe of the deity. To gaze at the yantra is to enter the temple of the goddess. Just as we have respect when entering a physical temple, when we enter this spiritual temple, we are entering the sacred field of Kali herself.

To invoke the *yantra* is to invoke the power, protection and activity of Kali. We can imagine it as though we are presenting ourselves and our lives to her. In turn, she imposes an energetic realignment that shifts, heals and recalibrates every aspect of what we offer to her, so it aligns with higher divine order. Whatever is missing for fulfilment is provided, and the yantra opens up an intermingling and integration between our personal field and the deity's field that cannot be undone. This is sacred and powerful work.

The downward-facing triangular formations in the centre of the yantra symbolise the regenerative power of the Divine Feminine. The colour red is the blood-red of life force, Kali's preferred fuel for destruction and rebirth. The grey represents the liminal, the medial, neither the black of night nor the brightness of day, but the place in-between. Although Kali is associated with waning moon cycles and darkest night, she is also a medial goddess, a soul doula, a birth and death mother, safely guiding us through the transitions and thresholds of our inner and outer lives. By invoking Ma through her yantra, we ask for her assistance in clearing the obstacles to progress and finding our way into what is next meant for us. It is the calling forth of the next chapter.

The subtle channels of energy unlocked through intentional engagement with yantra are further empowered through the placement of hands in postures, called *mudra*. The Kali mudra is created by interlocking your fingers and placing the left thumb over the right, with the index fingers together and extended to an upward-pointing position. The energy channels of the body are more readily permeated with Kali's essence of fearlessness and strength through assuming this posture.

This practice banishes interference, such as any negativity that would undermine your path and obscure your sacred fulfilment. The sacred fulfilment of the soul is in the best interests of all beings. We can grow through circumstances that may appear to be negative, but are later recognised as learning opportunities that provided the soul with valuable growth. Yet, once the learning has taken place, such energies need to be thoroughly released. If there are negative energies not necessary for growth—that would just make matters unduly complicated—they will be blocked. We do not need to know the extent of the Divine Mother's protection, nor even the nature of what she is protecting us from — all we need do is call upon her with pure-hearted trust. She will take care of all else.

Sacred Practice with Kali Yantra

Begin by opening your journal to the Kali Yantra image so you can see it easily and have your hands free to create the mudra when you are ready. If you are working with the *Kali Oracle*, you may like to work with the *Kali Yantra* oracle card.

Repeat her mantra eight times:

Om Krim Kalikayai Namaha.

(Sounds like, OHM KREEM CAR-LEE-KAI-YAY NAM-AH-HUH.)

Gaze at the image and place your hands at your heart, left over right. Gently begin to unfold your hands until both palms are facing upward as if you are making an offering from your heart to the Divine Mother as signified on the image. Imagine that you can connect with her from your heart directly through the image. See the offering move straight through the portal of the image to the spaciousness of the Divine Mother on the other side. As you do this, let there be softness, humility, reverence and purity in your heart. Repeat the movement three times offering love and peace from your heart.

Place your hands in the mudra. Bring your mind to focus gently upon what you wish to heal. You can express your request for healing in a prayer by saying:

> *Kali Ma, through divine grace for the spiritual benefit of all beings, I ask for healing with _____ and in all things according to your wisdom.*
> *Jai Ma! Jai Ma! Jai Ma!*

Focus on the image of the yantra and the mudra, then close your eyes and allow for her energy and blessings to fill you. Breathe out. Relax. Let it pour down and then expand outward through all aspects of your being. Let her presence infuse your being as though you are pure, clean water and she is deep, black, divine feminine tea seeping through your being, bringing blessing, healing, regeneration and protection. You may even feel you are stepping into the yantra, it now being a multidimensional experience of her divine being, infusing every cell and radiating all around you.

To increase the presence of Kali, for the benefit of all beings, finish with the following soft chant, repeated eight times:

> *Kali Ma Sohum.*

(Sounds like, CAR-LEE MA SO-HUM.)

Complete your sacred process by bowing your head with your hands in prayer at your heart.

You are allowed to receive wonderful blessings in your life.
If you have been enduring suffering, she is bringing it to an end.
She is ensuring you gain something of tremendous value from the
experience which will help you avoid suffering in future.

_Kali Ma, Dakshina Ma, I humbly bow before you. My heart leaps
with joy as I feel the presence of my soul's divine queen. I trust in you
to deliver your blessings, and in my capacity to receive, integrate and
heal through those blessings. For the spiritual benefit of all beings,
may I receive, receive and receive! Jai Ma Dakshina Kali!_

The skull indicates a need to acknowledge that while we are a powerful divine spirit with free will and much creativity, we also need to operate within the higher power of a far greater wisdom.

If going against divine wisdom is needed to keep something or someone in our lives, it can only create suffering. She will not only remove an impediment on your path but will support you so that releasing the attachment brings peace rather than endless sorrow.

*Trust your heart and don't be hesitant to lean into unfamiliar territory
with boldness tempered by patience.*

You will become capable of many things, on many levels, that you were not capable of accomplishing previously. A new way is signified.

At times, it can be hard to trust that everything is going to work out.
Yet we can trust, whether or not we see it coming, that divine love
shall always correct deficiencies and prevail.

_Allow for divine intervention to support you when battles take place
in your life or your mind. Should you sense that darkness is gaining
higher ground and your ability to trust in the face of the unknown is
being challenged, fear not. Have confidence that the tide of even the
most virulent negativity shall turn, swiftly and decidedly._

On abundance

Sometimes we pursue material items in an attempt to satisfy desires that require much more than material objects. Such desire could be for an experience of generosity, recognition, love, acceptance, joy, happiness or peace. Difficulties arise when we do not look to the deeper meaning for our pursuits, but become distracted or obsessed with material gain at any cost.

In such cases, we are out of balance and have lost connection with the profound healing wisdom guiding our path and reminding us to tune in to what holds real value. This is a balancing act with the complex drives that accompany the human condition. Material abundance and spiritual prosperity that are integrated and balanced can lead us into a place of peace and gratitude, soften the desire for more for the sake of it, and allow us to settle into flow.

Rather than under or overvaluing your material needs, recognise that life in a body on Earth is sacred. Your spiritual journey will be enhanced as you find your pathway to healing, peace and awakening — not only to the spiritual beauty of higher worlds but the divine beauty, healing and wisdom constantly expressing itself in the physical world. The Divine knows your life is meant to honour your spirit, and your spirit will honour and infuse your life with such radiance.

Trust that the Divine wants to heal and help you on every level.

Durga, mother of light and solar radiance of spiritual protection, I open to your divine blessing of Kali Ma, born of necessity, trusting that you shall accomplish all goodness, love and luminous wisdom. Jai Ma!

Although we may yearn for circumstances to unfold according to personally preferred timing, we must bow to the divine timing of a greater cycle. To trust in divine timing alleviates stress and fosters a more peaceful relationship with the Universe.

Persistence in clinging to what has been, the attachment to our past pain and fear of an unknown future are no match for her genius and unwavering will to clear away what is needed for the best conditions for the next chapter to unfold.

The tongue of Kali is a reminder that no matter what we may see unfolding
before us, there is always a pathway to the heroic and beautiful.

The Dark Mother will conquer the obstacles to your freedom with gentleness.
She will calm the waves of emotion, eradicate doubt and despair,
and provide safe and graceful passage through all difficulties.

Kali's presence in our being commandeers negative forces.
Instead of undermining us, we respond to those energies in such a way
that our peaceful inner light increases. We become increasingly skilful
at redirecting our focus to productive, healing pathways.

There is not always the need to try and grapple and conquer.
Sometimes, the need is simply to let go.

Just because another has created a reality for themselves and is attempting to draw you into it, there is no need for you to participate. You have the divinely imparted ability to choose where to invest your energy.

Kurukulla Shamanic Practice of Attraction and Enchantment for Swift Manifestation

A shamanic goddess adopted into later cultural traditions of Buddhism, Kurukulla is connected to Kali as one of the goddesses of her lunar cycle, called the *Kali Nitya*. Kurukulla is a medicine sorceress of enchantment, charisma and the manifestation of will. Hers is the realm of sacred spell-crafting and the power of attraction. She has one face, three eyes, four arms, and deep-red skin. Her semi-wrathful nature and her red skin are signs of her power to subjugate evil. Her red skin also signifies her power to attract and generate bliss, joy and passion. Her hooked sword overcomes negativity in all dimensions and from every direction. She is both a powerfully protective and joyfully creative divine being. Her bow and arrow symbolise her capacity to set us on the right course with precision, so our progress is swift and hits the mark like her arrow flying through the air.

A Kurukulla practice is especially powerful when we need to shift to a more passionately blissful way of being and need to overcome negative forces within and around us (cosmic party poopers!) to do so. She has the dual purpose of conquering any sabotaging, draining or otherwise negative energies *and* opening us to life. Thus, our receptivity is coupled with vitalising strength. For psychically sensitive persons who may feel anxious or vulnerable about being so open to life, lest they take on a whole lot of unwanted energy, Kurukulla is a precious gift. She creates the sort of openness that vitalises rather than overwhelms the soul.

This practice will support your wellbeing on a psychic level, boosting energy and clearing negative attachments. It will also help as you manifest your desires. Remember, always intend for your desires to manifest for the spiritual benefit of all beings. This way, you ensure that you are co-creating positive energy for all, rather than unintentionally creating obstacles for yourself or others. The relevant words are included in the following prayers for that reason.

A Note on Timing your Practice

It is best to do practices when you feel the time is right — which in a busy lifestyle may simply be when you get a moment to yourself! However, if you have the luxury of setting time aside, then calming practices are usually better in the evening, and more stimulating or energising practices like Kurukulla are better during the day. If you can combine an energising creative practice with a waxing moon, all the better. But, even if it is a waning moon, you could still do the work. Consider that the most auspicious time of day and month is supportive of the practice, but not necessarily essential. It is the state of your inner being, your intention and your heart that are the most powerful determinants of the success of a practice. I mention this here because if you choose to do this practice at night, you may have to discharge excess energy before you can fall asleep afterwards.

Ritual of Invocation

Take a deep breath in and exhale thoroughly to release. Repeat as many times as feels good for you, being sure to remain grounded and connected to yourself as you do so.

When you have completed your cleansing breaths, place your hand at your heart. Cultivate gratitude by focusing on what you have in your life that brings you joy — anything from a body that functions well to a person, talent, promise or vision. When you are in that grateful state, open your heart and mind to the possibility of receiving more. Let that be joyful for your heart, a chance to share more as a result. If you have fears that arise around this, they will pass away under Kurukulla's grace.

Visualise, intend, feel or pretend that there is a vibrant, ruby-red light shining in your heart. You may see two beautiful yellow eyes—like a wild cat's—shining out from the centre, and an opened third eye gleaming back at you. Perhaps you sense tiny fangs as her beautiful mouth curls into a smile. Here is Kurukulla in your heart.

As her gaze rests upon you, a secret pathway opens within your heart. This is a path of sacred passion, joy and bliss. Kurukulla is the threshold between the ordinary and the extraordinary, between the way things appear to be, and the divine potential for beauty to manifest according to higher wisdom. Sense the joy of this path. Allow that feeling to permeate and infuse your body and mind.

Say this prayer:

Kurukulla, beloved mother of attraction and subjugation, I invite your sacred protection and wisdom to manifest in my life for the spiritual benefit of all beings. May I gain release from the grip of falsehood and unworthiness, and open to receive that which you, in your grace, wish to bring to me. May all beings be liberated joyfully into your blissful nature! Jai Ma!

Stay focused on the gentle feeling of bliss and joy. It increases as you move along the sacred pathway toward a shining ruby-red Kurukulla temple, the body of the goddess. Imagine, feel or intend that exquisite and divine ruby-red light with golden threads is winding its way from the temple, through your heart, through your entire being, spreading her joyfulness, courage, bliss, blessings and protection. Let these energies wind their way out until they are free and coiling all around you, shining lights of gold and red that benefit all beings, in all dimensions. These healing lights continue to pulse outward, eternally energised from the divine temple of Kurukulla, accessed through your heart.

Repeat the following mantra as many times as you wish. Multiples of eight, nine or eleven are recommended. As you repeat the mantra, imagine, feel, intend and allow for the energy to build. As you speak the mantra, the energy of Kurukulla flows outward from the inner temple, riding the sound to manifest her divine will, protection and grace in the physical realm to benefit all beings.

Om Kurukulle Hri Soham, Om Tare Tam Swaha!

(Sounds like, OHM KOO-ROO-KOO-LAY HRI SO-HUM, OHM TAR-RAY TUM SWAH-HAH!)

Sense the sound and her lights of red and gold swirling around you. Allow her presence to become stronger, within you, and all around you, too. Now, say aloud:

For the spiritual benefit of all beings, may the Divine Mother's unconditional love, divine grace and spiritual protection manifest, now and always. Jai Ma!

Rest in this field of divine manifestation for as long as you wish. If you have a visualisation or spoken prayer that you wish to empower, you can do so, now. Remember to state at the end of any prayer or declaration:

… for the spiritual benefit of all beings.

When the time feels right, imagine, intend, feel or visualise that the powerful light, sound and manifestation of Kurukulla disperse, so that you are surrounded in a bubble of her spiritual blessing, and any excess energy intelligently goes to wherever it can do the most good.

Finish with your hands in prayer at your heart. You have completed your healing process.

Out of the fire of divine wrath your gentle form emerges,
calming the raging waves of emotion and disturbed fluctuations of the
mind. In settling myself beneath your fiercely compassionate
and tender gaze, I find steadiness, kindness and peace.

In this eternal moment with you, I am no longer afraid.

With humble mind and willing heart, I bow before you, ready to receive with gratitude, love and wonder at your divine beauty and kindness.

You are the unscripted creativity of the gentle, yet unyielding divine workings for the greatest good of all. Jai Ma Kali!

How do we proceed with trust? It is a choice we make.
When we sense the next step is before us, we proceed.
When we need to wait, we wait. We do not try to force,
but we tune in to our hearts and sense
what is guided in each moment.

It is protective compassion that prevents us from seeing anything other than the next one or two steps ahead of us. To know more is not always helpful, but when certain knowledge would support us on our path, we can be sure it will come to us.

On integrity

Do not turn away from your truths out of fear for what may come of them. Kali is spiritual integrity and right alignment. When you align yourself with spiritual integrity, you are aligning with her and you are held within her blessings of prosperity and protection. Reassure your mind that you will prosper on every level from living in integrity with your heart. There is nothing worthwhile, nor sustainable, that comes from living otherwise. Let this reassurance bring peace and trust to your heart. Kali knows the way through, and is with you even now, through endings and beginnings, so that the most vibrant spiritual fruition shall arise, according to the grace of her divine timing.

Attend to what you can now, leaving all else until the correct moment is upon you.
Your heart shall instinctively know when without needing to be told.

Acknowledging, "This is not good for me," or "I'm not yet sure what or how, but something needs to stop," sets healing in motion. An opportunity to end a difficult situation is arising. Embrace it.

You are learning how to self-protect and to have enough self-worth to realise you don't need to accept negative, undermining and toxic energies in your life. Your happiness and spiritual growth will increase as you clear them out.

There needs to be a healthy sense of self-worth to be committed to growth and learning. Believe that you are worthy of your destiny.

Do not be afraid to affirm your right to thrive.

She will never turn away from you. No matter what you have done,
no matter how many mistakes you have made, she is here for you, always.

Devotee of Kali Ma, the Hindu saint Sri Ramakrishna taught that when a tree is young, it should be fenced all around, lest it be destroyed by cattle.

There is something good growing within you. Don't let clumsy or
ill-wishing energies around or within you get anywhere near it!
Let Kali Ma protect you from within and without.

Devotional Prayer Dance for Gentle Kali to Heal and Bless Body, Mind and Soul

As a divine feminine being, Kali is responsive and creative in honouring the needs of our spiritual paths and earthly healing. There are many times when we can purposefully call upon her gentler side. We can trust that if her fierce nature is needed, that is how she will manifest for us. But, in cooing to her from our hearts, we also set an intention for peace and gentleness in our lives. Many souls find life tough. Hard work, intense challenges and devastating loss have honed the warrior within. While we can respect and honour the need for the warrior energy at the appropriate time, sometimes it is more helpful to settle into a more vulnerable, receptive and trusting space. This allows for a greater power to shoulder the burden as we 'let ourselves off the hook' from needing to figure everything out.

There is something profoundly healing, embodying and liberating about a gentle prayer dance. It doesn't require particularly fancy moves, or anything other than a willingness to breathe and move in whatever way feels authentic and the intention to offer it from the heart to the Divine. When we engage body, mind and energy in such a way, we participate with our entire being. It is a potent practice, yet one that can be soft and releasing in a gracious way. The catharsis we experience through such practice can be soft *and* powerful.

Bhadra Kali, or 'wish-fulfilling' Kali, is an auspicious and gentle form of Kali Ma. She is Kalyani who gives peace and happiness. She is the giver of boons, windfalls, blessings. Raksha Kali, without the protruding tongue so often associated with fiercer forms of Kali, has two arms, blue skin and a gentler expression. She brings protection from mass consciousness and lower energies, connecting us to a rich source of life-giving energies, inspirations and nourishment. As Shyama Kali, the peaceful blue goddess, she reminds us that it is not always effective to fight fire with fire it or to try to overcome force with greater force. Her wisdom is that of a gentling nature, able to calm, disarm and diffuse. There is not always a need to grapple and conquer. Sometimes, the need is simply to let go, to grow your ability to reorient yourself to the influences you choose with your own free will. If there is a mutual desire to connect and grow, then the path forward together can be more beautiful and healthy.

The simplicity of this wisdom can confuse those taught that they need to pick up any gauntlet thrown by any person at any time. This dance can be a release of the need to do that. You can embrace this process as an expression that you are strong enough to be gentle.

Ritual of Invocation

Find a private space where you can relax. This practice can be done with or without music. There are tracks of me singing to Kali on my *Voice of the Soul* and *The Kuan Yin Transmission™* albums, which you could use if you would like to play music during the movement offering of this process.

Say the following prayer:

> *Out of the fire of divine wrath, your gentle form emerges, calming the raging waves of emotion and disturbed fluctuations of the mind. In settling myself beneath your fiercely compassionate and tender gaze, I find steadiness, kindness and peace. In this eternal moment with you, I am no longer afraid. Bhadra Kali, Raksha Kali, Shyama Kali, my heart softens as I take delight in the realisation of your generosity and sweetness. With humble mind and willing heart, I bow before you, ready to receive with gratitude, love and wonder at your divine beauty. You are the unscripted magnificence of the gentle, yet unyielding divine workings for the greatest good of all. Jai Ma Kali!*

If you wish, you can now enhance your sacred ritual of invocation with a Kali dance — with or without music. You could also sing or speak repeatedly, over the music or with silence in the background, the following mantra:

Bhadra Kali, Jai Ma Kali.

Allow your body to move with gentle and loving expression. If other feelings arise, allow yourself to be authentic, to let your body express itself, rather than making it perform in a certain way. Your authentic expression may involve small flowing movements of your hands, graceful arcs of your arms, or your entire body moving or shaking. You may make small movements, large ones, or barely move at all, just swaying a little, back and forth. The point is to express what you feel within, not for it to look a certain way.

You can feel, intend or visualise that gentle shining-blue Kali is within your heart, a glorious sapphire goddess, shining her love and blessings. You could allow your arms and hands to express fluid, slow movements as you chant or move as if opening up to her presence with unconditional trust and love. You can finish your Kali prayer dance with your hands resting over your heart.

Take a moment to imagine, intend or visualise that the beautiful love and blessing you have begun to generate through your devotional prayer dance is shining as golden light within you. It reaches out in all directions and through all dimensions for the spiritual benefit of all beings. You are a beautiful light in the darkness, safe, steady, connected and secure in Kali's love and protection.

When you are ready, imagine sealing yourself in that light, in her presence. You are blessed and protected. You can place your hands in prayer and bow your head with thanks.

You have completed your sacred ritual of invocation.

It is natural for a child to need and reach for its mother.
You are deserving of comfort. Give yourself permission
to experience it without reservation.

*Supreme mother of the Universe, you and I are bonded in divine love,
a bond which can never be broken. May your comfort arise in my
heart now, reaching through all dimensions, for the spiritual benefit of
all beings. Jai Ma Kali!*

Certain inner processes need to take place beneath a cover of darkness,
privacy and sanctuary. You do not need to parade your process before
others, nor to prove anything to anyone.

You will sense when you are ready to put the sad days behind you and embrace the beginning of a happier time. No matter how unlikely that seems at this time, it will happen naturally as sure as spring follows winter.

We do not choose her. When we are ready, she chooses us.

Trust in that which feels right on an inner level. Do not allow a lack of external validation to deter you from your innate and authentic purpose.

*The strength of intention, combined with pure and fearless
commitment to your true nature, is enough to change the course of
what is happening in your being, in your life and in your world.*

Kali Mantra Shakti to Generate a Protective Field and Manifest Rapid Progress

There are times when patience is a virtue, and times when you know it is time to act. In such moments, you need to summon the strength and wisdom to act in such a way that spiritual benefit can be generated. It is not always easy to know how to do this. Our human perspective is limited, and our opinions or expectations can block our ability to hear and heed the inner knowing guiding us to take the action that will set our souls free. We can forget that what truly honours one soul brings benefit to all souls (even if certain egos complain at the time!).

To cut through obscurations and obstacles, within our mind and operating through external influences, we can invoke Kali. We give ourselves over to her energy flow, her direction and protection. We do so consciously and with the intention that spiritual benefits manifest for all beings through how we choose to live.

This practice increases the presence of Kali in our being and our lives. Thus, it is of benefit at any time and for any purpose. However, you can dedicate this practice to a specific healing, protection or understanding that you are seeking. Of course, Kali knows all. She knows what you need, and when. You may find that even though one matter calls you to the practice, you may emerge with clarity on other areas of your life, too.

The power of this practice directly correlates to the permission you give yourself to detach your thoughts and emotions from what has been, so you are free to immerse your attention in the process. This is the hardest part of any ritual, even harder than showing up in the first place! It is the moment of true surrender when you decide, *I am here, and I will experience this without hesitation or distraction.* How easy that is to attain will vary from day to day. We do not aim for perfection. We aim to engage with the process and be with what is.

Mantra is the use of sacred voice to shape the world, bring healing, and realign 'errors' in harmony with divine wisdom. It is an act of loving magic and powerful transformational healing. If you can hold the intention to emerge from your practice with a different consciousness to how you entered it, the effects of the work can be astonishing and continuing. Sound can bring harmony from chaos and create beautiful patterns for manifestations that are healing and enhancing of life. It can disrupt and break apart that which has been built. Sound is powerful. Sacred sound is power completely aligned with love and wisdom.

The sounds of Sanskrit mantra are said to have been handed down to humanity with the teachings of ancient *rishis* or 'sages' from the higher spiritual planes. They did so to help humans deal with the challenges they foresaw, still as relevant today as they must have been thousands of years ago. There are mantras for different purposes, and the simplest ones can be very powerful. There are 'seed sounds' or *bijas*, which are single-syllable mantras that evoke certain realities, including the realities or realms of various deities. The Kali bija is *Krim*. It sounds like, 'kreem'.

Krim is a sound for invoking the *shakti*, or 'power and activity', of Kali Ma in our lives and the world. It generates a powerful inner spiritual current, propelling the soul toward awakening. It breaks cycles of bondage. It aligns our will with hers, allowing the Divine Mother to direct us from within.

Sacred Practice of Mantra Shakti

Be seated or stand comfortably. Allow your awareness to settle on the flow of your breath, in and out. Move your jaw around in all directions to loosen tension subconsciously held there. To that end, you may also like to massage your head and face lightly. Rub across your neck, throat and the tops of your shoulders to bring awareness and release tension. Wiggle your shoulders. Can you breathe in and exhale more deeply, now too?

Sense your grounding and connection to the Earth beneath you and to your own body. Press your feet into the floor. If you cannot do this physically, for any reason, imagine you can do so energetically. Sense how your entire body is connected to the flow of breath.

Without becoming sleepy, relax your entire body as best you can. The breath flowing deeply in will help to energise you with alertness, and the breath flowing freely out will help you to relax.

When you are ready, say the following prayer:

Beloved Kali Ma Devi, I call upon the light — HREEEEMMMM — and I call upon your true nature — KREEEEMMMM. May the light bring peace and your true nature bring freedom. May there be perfect balance between calming and liberating forces. I lay claim to the creative divine power within me, and choose to align myself with the divine feminine power that protects, nurtures and liberates all beings with perfect wisdom. I trust in you, and speak your mantra, for the spiritual benefit of all beings. HREEEEEEEM. KREEEEEEEM. Jai Ma Kali!

Your mantra practice is outlined as follows:

The first mantra, *Hrim,* is the benefic mantra of light for the supreme feminine principle, the powerful originating mantra for the goddess. It brings light, calmness, positive energy and peace. It pacifies and protects from undue disturbance.

The second mantra, *Krim,* is the fierce sound of Kali Ma bringing absolute protection from negativity and the repulsion of invasive or interfering energies. Together, they are the complete protection of the Divine Feminine.

You can imagine, feel or intend that as you make these sounds, beautiful energies of divine feminine healing and power are gathering in your heart and then shining outward, in all dimensions for the spiritual benefit of all beings. The intention is not to force this process, but to allow those beings in need to be able to receive where this would be for their spiritual benefit. The intelligence within the sound knows how to accomplish this. Your job is to rest in your heart and have no attachment or intention beyond divine love as you make the sounds.

I suggest combining the above mantras into a group of three, as *Hrim, Krim, Hrim,* and reciting nine rounds, so a total of twenty-seven mantras are spoken. Nine is a sacred number. It symbolises a connection to the spiritual path and the desire for all beings to find spiritual peace, freedom and happiness. This number of repetitions resonates with the purpose of the practice.

HREEEEEMMMMMM.

KREEEEEMMMMMM.

HREEEEEMMMMMM.

When you have completed sufficient repetitions, rest with your hands at your heart.

You have completed your ritual of invocation.

Take only the steps you instinctively feel are correct at any time.
Even when your mind says, You must go this way or else you will fail, _let_
go of methods and strategies that do not truly resonate with your heart.

Kali Ma, Nirodha Shakti, you who still the incessant fluctuations of being and bring peace, I call upon your wisdom to break the cycles that need to be broken. I rest in you Ma, for the spiritual benefit of all beings. Jai Ma Kali!

When one sets a boundary, it is natural that there will be a time when others attempt to cross it. We do not need to feel fearful of this, but rather be wise to it. You have the divine birthright to choose how to deal with negativity.

If you have need of something, ask for it. Use your voice in a way that helps you
and empowers the Divine to help you, too.

Why not call for her daily to not only resolve issues but to prevent them from gaining traction in the first place? Your life can then become more peaceful for the spiritual benefit of all beings.